April 12, 2018

Donated to the
Society, for the love
of birds by,

David A. De Lemoine
Bx N.Y.

WORDS IN OUR BEAK, VOLUME TWO

As Told By Cam (A Female Cardinal)

With the Help of Patricia Youngquist, The Last Leaf Gardener

Patricia Youngquist,
The Last Leaf Gardener
+
"cam"

ISBN: 978–0–9963785–3–6

PRINTED BY

IngramSpark
1246 Heil Quaker Blvd.
La Vergne, TN 37086
www.ingramspark.com

Special Thanks to

CHRIS DEATHERAGE
for his editorial eye and graphic skills in the
layout design of this book series' print editions.

CDeatherage.Net
"Elegant, User–Friendly Web Design and Graphic Imaging"

WORDS IN OUR BEAK, Volume Two

is dedicated to the memory of

ELLEN MCCONNELL BLAKEMAN

(1954 — 2018)

Ellen was Cam's first fan and biggest supporter.
She will be missed, yet her fighting spirit lives on.
www.alongswim.org

A Long Swim is devoted to funding collaborative research for
amyotrophic lateral sclerosis (ALS), also known as Lou Gehrig's
Disease, and is a 501(c)(3) non–profit organization under
the U.S. Internal Revenue Code.

ALSO AVAILABLE

WORDS IN OUR BEAK, VOLUME ONE

As Told By Cam (A Female Cardinal)

With the Help of Patricia Youngquist, The Last Leaf Gardener

IngramSpark, ISBN 978–0–9963785–2–9

NOTE TO THE READER

Words In Our Beak, Volume Two continues the story told in the voice of Cam, a feisty and beautiful female cardinal living year–round in my New York City urban garden.

In this volume, Cam focuses less on people–ing (the term birds use when they observe humankind) and more on how natural and man–made changes to the garden affect both the birds who visit it and the flora that gives it life.

In the interim between Volume One and Volume Two, you will find that Cam has not become shy or lost her inclination to speak her mind. She has plenty to say about the unexpected events that interrupted her hobby of flora–ing (the term birds use to check out flora) and threatened her supply of black–oil sunflower seeds and peanuts. She also has quite a few choice comments about first–time avian visitors to her adopted home and community.

Cam's story continues to bring joy to her readers, as she does to me who is ever so grateful to "help" her give voice to the garden and its inhabitants.

Patricia Youngquist
The Last Leaf Gardener

Hi, there, dear reader! It's me, Cam! I'm back,

and it looks like you caught me here in TLLG's garden where I love to indulge in one of my favorite foods: black–oil sunflower seeds, which I raved about in Volume One of my book series.

And, as you can see, I still enjoy them . . .

. . . but I'm being reminded by other members of the avian community who often visite here to slow down with my munching!

It's time for me to fulfill my promise and tell you what occurred within the rooftop garden where I've been living.

And I fully intend to do this — after I grab a peanut or two — for as you may recall, I enjoy eating them too!

Ok, now that I've had some food to feed my thought, I'm ready to pick up where I left off in Volume One and begin Volume Two.

But first let me make a confession, and that is to let you know my delay in finishing this particular volume stems from the fact that my children — Frannie, Vincenzo, and Pica–John — begged me to take them on a vacation.

All of them accused me of spending too much time on my writing instead of being with them.

 My son Vincenzo said I was being somewhat hypocritical, given that I had made such a point (in my first book) of stressing that time spent with one's child is fleeting, and therefore it must be embraced on as many occasions as possible.

Frannie and Pica–John piped up with arguments of their own.

Frannie said that it had been such a long time since they had gotten to visit their cousins that we must go to the beach. She said it so sweetly and innocently, mind you, I suspect her real reason was wanting to chase after male cardinals. Like her mother, she wants them "the redder the better," but I only have eyes for my Mac, and Frannie is still too young to get serious with a male cardinal.

Pica–John, who is afraid of missing out on everything her sister gets to do, stomped her foot and declared that "if Frannie gets to go, I get to go too!"

Mac and I talked over taking the kids on a vacation, and we decided that going to the beach to visit the cousins was a good idea and that Mac would stay behind to make sure certain songbirds — I'm not naming any names — didn't take over the feeders in TLLG's garden. Being a true "daddy's girl," little Peanut stayed home with him.

[FYI, just as I did in Volume One, I will be referencing Patricia Youngquist, The Last Leaf Gardener, as "TLLG" here too. I will also be referring to her gardening comrade — also introduced in Volume One — as Juan V (but I won't be mentioning him just yet).]

Apparently I was wrong about my children's motives because it turned out that their cousins had been sending them photos (via Snapchat) of American oyster catchers *[Haematopus palliatus]*.

The cousins had eagerly read my book, Words In Our Beak, Volume One, and they thought that if beaks were of interest to me, I "*should see the beaks of a bird type known as the American oyster catcher, especially since the coloration of this bird's beak is similar to Aunt Cam's*" (as evidenced from their photographs).

American oyster catchers frequently will walk or run rather than fly. When they walk across shellfish beds and encounter one that is partially open, they jab their bill into the shell and sever the strong muscle that clamps the shells shut. Shellfish, when caught unawares, are no match for American oyster catchers and their their long blade–like bills.

The American oyster catchers' technique of jabbing their bills into a fish's shell to open it reminded me of how blue jays and we cardinals use our beaks to open peanut shells that are procured from feeders in TLLG's garden.

However, cracking shells open is not without its risks for the American oyster catcher. Cornell states that "*Oyster catchers sometimes drown after a tightly rooted mussel clamps down on their bills and holds the bird in place until the tide comes in.*" The American Oyster catcher seems to live life to the fullest with enjoyment (below) — in spite of that danger.

American oyster catchers share a habit with the many other types of shore birds, as well as of the wild birds whom I've met in TLLG's garden: They stand on one leg.

Why all birds do this is because bird's legs have a unique system of blood veins, called **rete mirabile** (pronounced "***ree**-tee meh-**rah**-bi-lay*"), that minimizes heat loss. Here is how it works: The arteries that transport the warm blood from the heart into the legs lie in direct contact with the veins that return colder blood back to

the bird's heart, so the warm blood heats the cooler blood. Standing on one leg and pulling the other leg up against the warmth of its body allows a bird to reduce the amount of heat loss by up to half. In short, they stand on one leg to warm up a little bit.

While we were away, Mac took Peanut to Central Park to watch a family of geese *[Branta canadensis]* for, as you may recall, dear reader, Central Park is very near TLLG's garden.

Peanut was really moved by how both male and female geese care for their goslings, and she took the following sequence of photographs:

Now that I've caught you up on what's been happening with my family and me, back to Volume Two without further ado!

To recap, at the end of Volume One, we had left TLLG's garden for our vacation, only to discover upon our return that the once lush garden where we had been living was almost barren!

Mac and Peanut had not wanted to tell me, Frannie, Vincenzo, or Pica–John about the garden for fear that knowing it would ruin our vacation. That was very sweet of them, but I was still very distressed as to what had happened to all the flora!

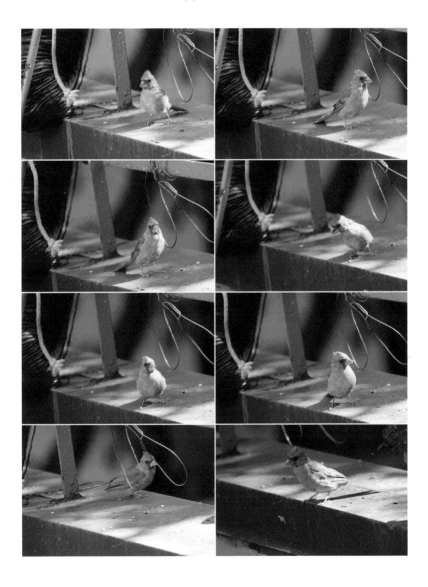

If you look closely at the aerial view of the barren garden, you will notice two mourning doves *[Zenaida macroura]*, bird types that were discussed in my first book.

One is alighting atop the bare branches of the kiwi vines *[Actinidia arguta]* that wrap around the railing of TLLG's garden (seen in the mid–to–right portion of the image), and the other mourning dove is on the floor of the garden.

I mentioned in Volume One that the mourning doves would be able to tell me what had occurred here. And they did not disappoint!

The doves reported that TLLG had to move all her containers of flora off the garden surface and put them inside her living space because the landlord who owns the building wanted to replace her garden's "floor!"

Since TLLG's living space measures seventeen feet by five feet and eight inches — and her garden measures nine feet across and seventeen feet in length — this was no easy feat!

These pictures give you a sense of what the inside of TLLG's home looked like after the "move in:"

In the same barren garden image where I pointed out the mourning doves, there are three black contractor bags tied to the railing that surrounds TLLG's garden. One bag is inset inside the orange circle and is actually off–camera.

The Number One contractor bag was placed over some of the foliage and flowers of a *Pancalata Clematis*.

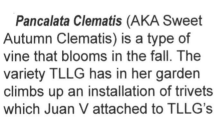

Pancalata Clematis (AKA Sweet Autumn Clematis) is a type of vine that blooms in the fall. The variety TLLG has in her garden climbs up an installation of trivets which Juan V attached to TLLG's garden wall many years ago. Annually, this vine produces hundreds of little white flowers.

In TLLG's garden, the Autumn Clematis [*Clematis terniflora*] grows in the southeast corner. The vine's box–style container is on the garden floor, and the vine trails up Juan V's trivets, as seen in the photo, above. Its empty container can be seen below, with my "informant," the mourning dove, alighting atop of it:

The soil for the Autumn Clematis had been taken inside TLLG's home! And, as I've said, the vine that had been planted in this container was wrapped in the contractor bag (seen in the pictures below, and is "Number One" in the first image on page 23).

The Number Two bag on the page 23 top image protects another one of TLLG's vines, which is known as an H. F. Young Clematis *[Ranunculaceae]*. Under "normal" circumstances, this is a vine which grows in the northwest corner of the garden. To prepare for the "renovation," this vine's container, along with the soil, were also taken inside TLLG's home!

The H.F. Young Clematis blooms in May, bearing big purple blooms that trail up a permanent "utility" pole in that corner of the garden. The next set of images — taken prior to the "renovation" — feature its humongous buds and brilliant flowers. Even when the petals drop, what remains of the flowers is stunning!

By the way, the H.F. Young had been planted in TLLG's garden at least seven years prior to the need to empty its container and place what remained in a contractor bag in order to clear the garden for the renovation. Therefore, the vine's root–ball was massive and had to be chopped with a hacking–style garden tool before "tucking it away."

This particular clematis is known to be "Queen of the Vines," and I don't imagine a queen enjoys the "accommodations" of a contractor bag!

A lone female house finch *[Haemorhous mexicanus]* truly missed the H.F. Young Clematis flowers and spent time on the pole where that vine once thrived trying to determine where the buds, as well as all the flowers, had gone (photo, left).

Evidently (according to my sources, the pair of mourning doves), the birds who were on the scene during the bagging of the vines, also witnessed the kiwi vines being upended from their container home and placed in a bag (refer to Number Three on the page 23 top photo and in close–up, at right).

In this garden, the branches of the kiwi vines are normally grown in a place that many of the birds who visit can enjoy as a place to perch (including me, as well as the female and male house finches, respectively).

Mourning doves (above) also enjoy alighting upon the kiwi vines. They told me that they even perched near to the kiwi vines' branches when they were bundled into a contractor bag (right).

[The kiwi vines are somewhat famous in this garden, because one of them narrated a movie produced by TLLG. It's called *The Kiwi Speaks! Fifteen Minutes of Fame...almost*, and can be viewed on Vimeo via this link: https://vimeo.com/37027072.]

TLLG tells me these vines have been growing here for at least ten years. And when the vines' branches are bare, the neighboring gardens are exposed through the railings . . .

. . . but since the container that houses them is on the garden floor, and the garden floor had to be "renovated," the container had to be moved inside while the contractor bag was filled with soil from the kiwi vines' container.

I prefer to remember the kiwi vines when they are just beginning to bud for a given season; as you can see they produce buds that quickly turn into small leaves!

The vines are as lush with green foliage in spring and summer as they are during the fall when their leaves have turned yellow with red markings.

The vines' branches can also be seen covered with snow when they are wrapping around most of the railing that surrounds this garden.

But I've digressed by giving you so many de-tails about the kiwi vines that were put in contractor bags! Once all the flora was moved inside or tied to the railing, TLLG was informed that the entire sur-face of the garden floor had to be ripped up and replaced!

TLLG realized that removing the floor would make us lose our "dining room," so she placed a tray with seeds atop of it, on the bare garden deck. The mourning doves were happy to dine there, and at one point a lone house finch even joined them for dinner.

I've often said that New York City is the place to be if you are a bird, but the scenario regarding TLLG's garden "renovation" has made me question if it's really the place to be if one has a rental apartment with a garden!

I'm saying this because TLLG's landlord did not order any materials (he wanted to reuse what was there), and when he discovered that nothing was reusable, he told her it would be days before the proper new materials arrived!

Because TLLG did not want her outdoor flora to be traumatized by being in her dark apartment, she brought everything outside and placed it on a drop cloth until the expected delivery arrived!

Fortunately for us birds, TLLG still continued to provide for us by putting black–oil sunflower seeds atop trays on stands in the garden. Her efforts to accommodate the birds who visited here were not wasted on me!

House finches also indulged in the black–oil sunflower seeds from the tray, which should've come as no surprise to me (or to you, dear reader) given what I wrote in Volume One about them indulging in these seeds. What did come as a surprise to me was that it was mostly the male house finches who arrived to eat. It was rare that a female house finch showed up.

But who am I to judge why mostly male house finches came to dine during the so–called renovation, while the females (for the most part) didn't come around.

Some birds don't deal well when things are not orderly. My husband, Mac, is one of them, and so are my kids! None of them spent time here during the garden upheaval, even though there were plenty of black–oil sunflower seeds to be had!

On the other hand, mourning doves like me are more adaptable and roll with the punches, especially if that means being able to eat our favorite foods! Both male and female mourning doves often showed up alone to dine during the garden's upending.

And yet on a number of occasions rather than come alone, they came as a couple or brought their children. Moreover, the adult mourners even taught their little ones some dining manners in the midst of the garden chaos!

Prior to the "renovation," — besides my family and myself — house finches and mourning doves were the only bird type to visit this garden. That is until . . .

. . . a lone blue jay *[Cyanocitta cristata]* showed up. I confess that I was not able to determine if this particular jay was male or female. This is because both sexes of this bird type share the same plumage. Male blue jays tend to be larger in size than females, but it is difficult to tell them apart by size alone. Careful observation of courtship and nesting behavior is the best way to tell their sexes apart, and I obviously could not do that when I

first noticed the blue jay I'm describing here. So, for purposes of this narrative, I will refer to this bird type with feminine pronouns.

One can be seen spying on us while perched upon one of TLLG's urban hedges in the photo above.

"Urban hedge" is a term TLLG uses when referring to a human–made fence as opposed to one comprised of more traditional flora such as juniper, yew, boxwood, or holly. The urban hedge on which this blue jay alights here is made of bamboo sticks that have been anchored in planting pots sitting atop the ledges surrounding TLLG's garden.

Over the years, TLLG explained that she had experimented with different flora in these pots. She shared with me several of her pic-tures featuring the bamboo stick urban hedge when honeysuckle *[Lonicera]* trailed upon it. I'm including a few on the next page.

I learned that the honeysuckles did not do too well in this environment. TLLG and Juan V had to swap them out for a vine known as a Cardinal Climber *[Ipomea horsfalliae]*, which I was happy about given the vine being named for my bird type, albeit for the male variety.

However, since the Cardinal Climber is an annual, it had to be swapped for a perennial at the end of the growing season. TLLG and Juan V chose beautiful climbing white roses *[Rosa hybrid Iceberg]*. After the garden was restored, they also replaced the bamboo urban hedge with a solid wood trellis to support the roses.

But, I have digressed and gotten ahead of myself, as I often tend to do! Getting back to that lone blue jay alighting on the trellis (which was bamboo at the time), I suspect she might've discovered TLLG's garden when she was people–ing from the vantage point of a perch on a rooftop or railing of a neighboring building.

There are plenty of buildings that can offer a bird someplace to perch while checking out the surrounding area, as you can see in the following picture where I had TLLG draw an orange circle around TLLG's garden.

And details of places where fauna can go to get a bird's eye view of TLLG's can be seen in this set of images:

Then again perhaps the jays did not discover TLLG's garden from buildings! They may have seen it from a vantage point of nearby trees.

Be that as it may, jays are unshelled peanuts lovers — like yours truly! And had I made a bet when they discovered TLLG's garden that I would now have competition at the peanut feeders, I would've won. From the time they first began visiting, a jay would always be at an unshelled peanut feeder in TLLG's garden!

But getting back to my story . . . .

Once the so–called renovation was complete, TLLG's garden began to come back to its "normal" state. And she was even able to decorate the garden for Halloween! The left photo below shows a partial view of the garden's comeback. If you look closely, you will see a bit of Halloween décor hanging on the bamboo urban hedge at the left side of the image. (I asked TLLG to draw circles and arrows on the lower right photo showing more of the garden in order to point out where the Halloween decorations are.)

The larger black oval references the Halloween décor on TLLG's garden shelving unit, which she often regards as another urban hedge. It is another favorite perching place in the garden, as you can see when an avian newcomer, called a tufted titmouse *[Baeolophus bicolor],* came by to check out the Halloween decorations.

Just as it is with blue jays, differentiating between male and female titmouses is hard to discern, as both sexes look pretty much alike. Some subtle distinctions between the two, however, give hints regarding gender. Both tufted titmouse sexes have gray bodies with orange or buff underparts and a small crest, or tuft, on the head. They also have black forehead patches, which you might need binoculars to see clearly.

Since it's tough to tell their gender difference based on sight, one has to watch and listen to these little birds to figure it out. Not only are these birds attracted to feeders, but they will raise their young in backyard nest boxes if a person provides them. That gives folks (and any observant birds) the opportunity to see the behavior of these lifelong breeding pairs and figure out which is which. Before anyone spots the hen sitting on eggs, the male can be heard singing his courtship songs.

[I'm sorry to say I was never able to confirm the gender of the tufted titmouses within the confines of TLLG's garden, so I'll just refer to them as "she," as I have for the blue jays.]

While the tufted titmouse was checking out the garden's Halloween decorations, she naturally partook of some black–oil sunflower seeds from TLLG's umbrella feeder sitting on the top level of the shelving unit. (I wrote about that feeder in Volume One.)

Now referring back to my diagram of the Halloween décor, the smaller black oval in the upper right indicates the pumpkin string lights dangling from the bamboo urban hedge. Another tufted titmouse seemed curious about those pumpkin–shaped lights.

The black arrow (*cf.* in the bottom right photo, page 40) is indicating flowers from TLLG's Autumn Clematis that have crawled up the trivet–installation wall which I described earlier. Everyone was grateful that this vine continued to thrive in spite of the upheaval in the garden during the enforced renovation.

And the orange arrow in my diagram points to Halloween décor that's placed in the area off camera:

Halloween seems to be a big deal in NYC. There is a famous parade in the West Village, but as I told readers in Volume One, I tend to stay inside a small radius within my neighborhood and that is why I was somewhat hard pressed to take our Long Beach vacation with my children.

In any event, my tendency to stay nearby is a typical habit of people who live in NYC, or at least in my area, which is why I don't go to the West Village to see the annual Halloween parade.

Besides, there is so much going on in NYC during Halloween that there is plenty to see without going downtown. In fact, many people decorate their brownstone façades . . .

. . . while oth-
ers decorate the
trees next to their
brownstones.

There are some
who create a Hal-
loween atmosphere
just by decorating
pumpkins and plac-

ing them on the sidewalk or on the on the stoop of their homes.

I have a word of warning to folks who decorate for Halloween. I advise you not to put up fake spider–webs, or other decorations made of entangling fibers, as they can be hazardous for us birds. Wild birds can easily get trapped and not be able to break the material to free themselves.

Moreover, anything that dangles or flutters is also a potential hazard. Avoid decorations with loops or closed circles. A foraging animal or bird can inadvertently put his head through one of those loops or circles and choke herself.

But there I go again, digressing, even if it is about Safety First!

Now that TLLG's garden was making its comeback, she set about, as she does every year, including a couple of Jack–O–Lanterns, who always enjoy themselves.

I hope she knows how much I enjoy the festive spirit she gives to the garden, but this year's celebration of a "back to normal garden" and the presence of the smiling Jack–O–Lanterns was cut short by the arrival of Superstorm Sandy.

This massive storm started ominously in New York City. The President had issued an emergency declaration regarding the state of New York late the night before. School was cancelled across the city. A pre–storm surge had already caused severe flooding in the Red Hook and Gowanus neighborhoods of Brooklyn, New York, two areas where TLLG has shopped for herbs, flowers, plants, shrubs, trees, and vines.

The New York Stock Exchange shut down. The subways, too. Bridges were closed. So were the airports. There was a mandatory evacuation order for everyone in low lying areas. That afternoon, the wind even caused a construction crane on a midtown skyscraper to collapse. New York City's mayor claimed that Sandy was the "storm of the century" and that the time to evacuate was "over."

While Sandy largely spared most New York neighborhoods, it devastated others all along the coastal areas. Over eight million New Yorkers all have different memories from that fateful night, when Sandy's record storm surge slammed against the city's shores, causing billions of dollars in damage, plunging parts of the city into darkness, and ultimately killing forty–three people.

My memory of the event is this: TLLG had to bring most of the containers — with the herbs, flowers, plants, trees, and, shrubs still in them — inside her apartment! She also had to bring in any outdoor accessories or furniture that could not be tied down. So, once again the lush garden, which serves as a safe haven for my family and me as well as our other bird friends, was again in a state of disarray!

TLLG was concerned about the safety of us birds during a storm like this, and she came up with a way to secure certain birdfeeders in order to insure her avian community would still have access to food during the storm.

What TLLG did was to remove a plant holder from the ledge surrounding her garden and place it upside down on the floor, nearer to her building's exterior wall. Then, she put various feeders underneath it and saw to it that they were firmly secured by the plant holder.

My husband Mac was one of the first avian creatures to dine from this "system," which surprised me, for as I told you, he does not care to eat in disruptive surroundings! He even grabbed the crumbs that fell alongside of it!

And the tufted titmouse took advantage of the umbrella feeder after it was tied down securely in anticipation of the predicted high winds tfrom the impending superstorm.

But the umbrella style feeder was certainly not the only thing which had to be secured during the storm prep. TLLG's bouncer chair had to be put on its side and tied down to prevent it from blowing away. A lone tufted titmouse clearly didn't mind the chair being on its side: she used it as a perching spot.

And just as it was during the aftermath of the so–called renovation, when it came to noshing at TLLG's "Super Sandy Feeding System," the male finches outnumbered the females.

There was a newcomer who arrived during Superstorm Sandy, and that's a White–Throated Sparrow *[Zonotrichia albicollis]*. The weather conditions made it nearly impossible to get decent images of this creature, but TLLG and I recognized the type by the yellow markings near this bird's eye.

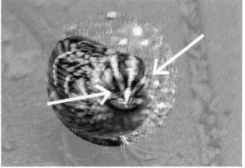

That was the first time TLLG and I had ever noticed a White–Throated Sparrow in the garden, and it was also the last! Evidently, White–Throated Sparrows spend most of their time in Central Park, which is fine by me, as it means less competition for black–oil sunflower seeds!

But I do admit the White–Throated Sparrow is quite striking, and fortunately for your viewing pleasure, I can share some pictures of them that TLLG took while roaming in Central Park.

I'm thankful to report that Superstorm Sandy did not damage TLLG's garden! My avian community and I were able to enjoy spending time there in the aftermath of Sandy, but it was short lived!

For yet another event occurred — just six days after Sandy — causing a third garden upheaval. A powerful nor'easter helped provide just enough cold air to dump more than a foot of snow in the tri–state area of Connecticut, New Jersey, and New York!

Once again, TLLG's garden was upended to prepare for this November nor'easter. Plants and pots were stored inside the apartment while the bird feeders were secured to keep food available to all of us birds.

The garden ultimately did receive more than a foot of snow, but it was what you would call a wet snow and melted very soon after. And wouldn't you know the first avian creature to take advantage of the situation was a blue jay!

To tell you the truth, I'm not sure if she's the one I wrote about earlier (at the tail–end of the garden's surface renovation saga), or if this was a different jay altogether. Yet, there was that lone blue jay, dining on seeds from the replenished feeders.

In the weeks that followed those storms, a dark–eyed junco *[Junco hyemalis]* began to visit TLLG's garden.

The junco is another bird type whose gender is not easily determined. (One certainty can't say that about us cardinals!) When it comes to juncoes, females tend to stand more upright, with head held high and body higher above the ground, and they have a thinner neck, whereas the male has bulging neck feathers.

Females tend to show a very slight crest, while the males' crown profile is more rounded. Females are lower on the pecking order

and are often chased by males, leading to more active and fidgety movements. (For the purpose of my story, I will refer to the dark–eyed juncoes with feminine pronouns because we girls must stick together.)

In any event, I'm not certain if this dark–eyed junco's visit was a result of bird migration being affected by the storms (since I don't migrate) or, if this creature just happened to discover the garden in a similar manner that the other birds who have been coming here had found "our" place.

And this junco was not particularly sociable, so I couldn't ask how she found TLLG's garden. Dark–eyed juncoes are winter birds though, so it's not that unusual one came at this time of year.

The junco is a ground feeder, like yours truly and my husband Mac. She wasted no time making herself at home near the storm–secured feeders which Mac had been enjoying during Superstorm Sandy.

Furthermore, the little gal got cozy in the container of TLLG's *Pyracantha coccinea*, which you might remember is a favorite spot for female house finches if you have read Volume One.

In the days following the nor'easter, the fall season became quite beautiful throughout the city, and

TLLG's garden was no exception. This fact may have caused the junco to bring other members of her family to spend time here.

Additionally, the tufted titmouse (who I mentioned first appeared near the time frame of Superstorm Sandy), began visiting in TLLG's garden on a regular basis once all the consequences of the aftermath of that storm, as well as the aftermath of the nor'easter, had settled down.

The tufted titmouse has a reputation of being as perky as a chickadee *[Poecile atricapillus]*. In fact, it's a cousin to the chickadee. And it wasn't too long before one of the titmouse's cousins showed up in TLLG's garden.

I thought that a lone mourning dove seemed to be quite awestruck by this chickadee's physical looks, and you might come to the same conclusion upon seeing the picture on the right.

However, I soon realized that the mourning dove was not gazing at this chickadee out of an admiration for the crea-

ture's beauty. What she was actually thinking was of a way to gain access to the feeder at the same time as the chickadee perched there. As you can see in the picture, left, the dove managed to get to the seeds through the back door.

House sparrows *[Passer domesticus]* also began to visit TLLG's garden on a frequent basis. Prior to this time, the only sparrow variety who had visited here was a lone representative from that White–Throated sparrow family, who showed up during the time of Superstorm Sandy.

And with the arrival of house sparrows, I had more competition than ever in procuring the black–oil sunflower seeds that TLLG filled in her bird feeders, and even for those that fell to the garden's floor.

Judging from how comfortable house sparrows seemed to be in TLLG's garden, as evidenced by this one enjoying the fall foliage of TLLG's kiwi vines, it looked like they would probably stick around for quite some time.

Before the house sparrows could secure squatters' rights, there was another disruption in the normal routine of TLLG's garden. However, this one wasn't brought on by the landlord renovating, nor by Mother Nature. No, this one was man–made!

All of a sudden, it was time for Juan V and TLLG to begin their annual ritual of winterizing the garden, which meant that every container "housing" a given flora has to be wrapped in bubble wrap. After this task was completed, layers of burlap had to be placed over the bubble wrap and then tied with jute.

[TLLG produced a mini movie regarding the process of winter-izing a garden which she and Juan V use. The feature, titled *It's a Wrap! Bubble Wrap!*, can be viewed at this link, https://vimeo.com/35987813, on her Vimeo channel.]

And on that cliffhanger, I conclude Volume Two. But before I do, I must apologize for not introducing you to several of the garden's avian visitors as promised at the end of Volume One. I am proud to say that I'm on a first name basis with three of them . . .

. . . Wilson, a member of the Rose–Breasted Grosbeak Family *[Pheucticus ludovicianus]*;

. . . Emily, a member of the Baltimore Oriole family *[Icterus galbula];*

. . . and Harper, a Northern mockingbird *[Mimus polyglottos]*;

. . . nor will I ever be able to forget these first time visitors who belong to . . .

. . . the Downy Woodpecker family *[Picoides pubescens]*;

. . . the Common Grackle family *[Quiscalus quiscula]*;

. . . the White–Breasted Nuthatch family *[Sitta carolinensis]*;

. . . or the entourage of pigeons *[Columbidae]*;

. . . and the array of European starlings *[Sturnus vulgaris]*.

In my defense for leaving them out of Volume Two, I found that recounting all the upheavals of the garden was much harder to relive than I anticpated, and I swear — standing on a mound of black–oil sunflower seeds — that I'll faithfully tell you their stories in Volume Three.

Also in Volume Three, I plan to include tales of other bird types who have since showed up in TLLG's garden (in order of their appearance):

. . . members of the American Goldfinch family [*Spinus tristis*];

. . . members of the American Robin family *[Turdus migratorius]*;

. . . and a lone house finch who is leutistic;

. . . as well as a lone American Kestrel *[Falco sparverius]*.

And of course, I will give you an accounting of how TLLG's flora fared in their winterized state and were more than ready for a spring fling.

Yikes! Now that I have re–read my outline for Words In Our Beak, Volume Three, I realize I need to start dictating it ASAP because as you will recall, dear reader, TLLG is a hunt–and–peck typist who can barely keep up with the words in my beak. So, pardon my back again; time for me to fly!

(But first, I'd better re-fuel with some peanuts and black–oil sunflower seeds for dessert.)

An AFTERWORD from CAM

Oops, before I grab another bite to eat . . .

I want to thank you for buying and reading my books. I do so love sharing my story with you (thanks to TLLG!), and I am grateful for all the kind words you have said and written about them.

Because I feel bad that I had to end Volume Two where I did (and make you wait for Volume Three to finish my story), I decided to share with you some of my favorite photographs that I wasn't able to include in Volume Two. There were just too many to choose from! So why, I thought, shouldn't you enjoy as many as you can? (Peanut, who likes to take photos, agreed with me!)

Hope you enjoy my little "bonus" photo album. See you again in Volume Three!

Cam

Patricia Youngquist, The Last Leaf Gardener, is a visual artist and writer whose work seamlessly moves between the disciplines of photography, blogging, and videography.

Starting with her emotionally impressionistic black–and–white photography that evolved into her colorful prismatic kaleidoscopics created with a pinhole camera of her own design, Patricia's photography now focuses on the lushly realistic flora and fauna of her urban garden and sharp, intimate close ups of the birds and insects who visit it.

As a blogger, Patricia uses simple and accessible verbiage to paint vividly descriptive mental images, a skill that is translated into her lyrical videos which celebrate moments in time. To experience the full depth of Patricia's work please visit:

http://www.patriciayoungquist.com

http://www.thelastleafgardener.com

https://vimeo.com/133713841

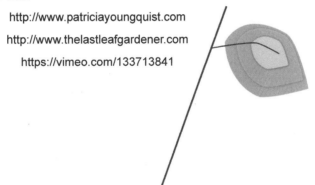

CPSIA information can be obtained at www.ICGtesting.com
Printed in the USA
BVIW12n0149090418
512832BV00010B/47